Barracudas

A Buddy Book by
Deborah Coldiron

ABDO
Publishing Company

UNDERWATER WORLD

VISIT US AT
www.abdopublishing.com

Published by ABDO Publishing Company, 8000 West 78th Street, Edina, Minnesota 55439.

Copyright © 2009 by Abdo Consulting Group, Inc. International copyrights reserved in all countries. No part of this book may be reproduced in any form without written permission from the publisher. Buddy Books™ is a trademark and logo of ABDO Publishing Company.

Printed in the United States.

Coordinating Series Editor: Sarah Tieck
Contributing Editor: Michael P. Goecke
Graphic Design: Deborah Coldiron
Cover Photograph: Brandon Cole Marine Photography
Interior Photographs/Illustrations: Brandon Cole Marine Photography (pages 13, 15, 17, 23, 25); iStockphoto.com: Chris Bishop (page 28), Taylor Fulde (page 29), Marian Todd (page 30); Minden Pictures: Chris Newbert (page 17), Norbert Wu (page 27); Photos.com (pages 5, 7, 9, 16, 17, 19, 21); SeaPics.com (page 16)

Library of Congress Cataloging-in-Publication Data

Coldiron, Deborah.
  Barracuda / Deborah Coldiron.
    p. cm.-- (Underwater world)
  Includes index.
  ISBN 978-1-60453-129-9
  1. Barracudas--Juvenile literature. I. Title.

QL638.S77C65 2008
597'.7 -- dc22

                             2008005043

Table Of Contents

The World Of Barracudas

Every living creature needs water. Some animals not only need water, they live in it, too.

Scientists have found more than 250,000 kinds of plants and animals living underwater. And, they believe there could be one million more! The barracuda is one animal that makes its home in this underwater world.

Water covers 70 percent of Earth's surface.

Barracudas are long, thin fish. They have large heads and forked tails. Large, sharp teeth fill their mouths.

Barracudas live mostly in **tropical** areas of the ocean. Some live in **temperate** waters, too.

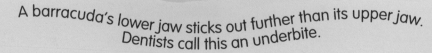

Barracudas cannot survive in freshwater. They can live only in salty ocean water.

There are more than 20 barracuda **species**. Most have gray skin and pale, silver bellies. Some have dark spots or patterns on their sides.

FAST FACTS

The largest barracuda ever caught with a hook and line was more than five feet (2 m) long. It weighed 103 pounds (47 kg)!

The largest and most well-known barracuda is the great barracuda. They can be six feet (2 m) long and weigh 100 pounds (45 kg).

A Closer Look

The barracuda is famous for its two rows of teeth. Outside its mouth is a short, razor-sharp set. These teeth slash and cut prey.

Inside a barracuda's mouth is a longer set of teeth. These teeth help trap prey.

FAST FACTS A barracuda has holes in its jaws to give its long teeth a place to go. Without them, a barracuda could not close its mouth!

The Body Of A Barracuda

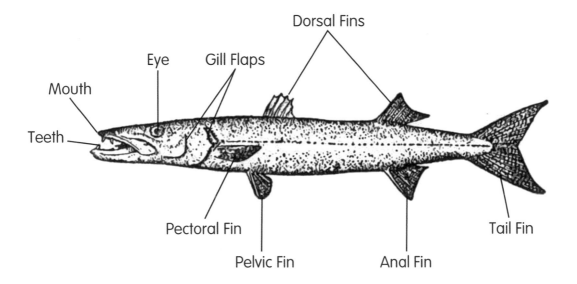

A Growing Barracuda

Scientists do not know where or when barracudas **spawn**. They do know that females release eggs into open water. And, males **fertilize** them there.

The eggs drift off with the currents. Then, the eggs hatch. Barracuda larvae (LAHR-vee) grow and develop in the open ocean.

Divers often see groups of barracudas in the open ocean. But, no one has ever seen barracudas spawn in the wild.

After the larval stage, young barracudas seek shelter while they continue growing. As they get even larger, they leave their hiding places for open water.

Male barracudas reach adulthood at about two years old. Females become adults around four years of age.

FAST FACTS

Scientists cannot identify if a live barracuda is male or female.

14

Young barracudas find shelter in sea grass beds. Adults visit sea grass beds to hunt.

Family Connections

Barracudas belong to the Sphyraenidae (sfuh-REE-nuh-dee) family. There are more than 20 barracuda **species** in this group.

Barracudas do not have any close relatives. So, there are no other fish within the family.

Great barracudas are curious and sometimes follow divers. These giants can be identified by black spots on their sides.

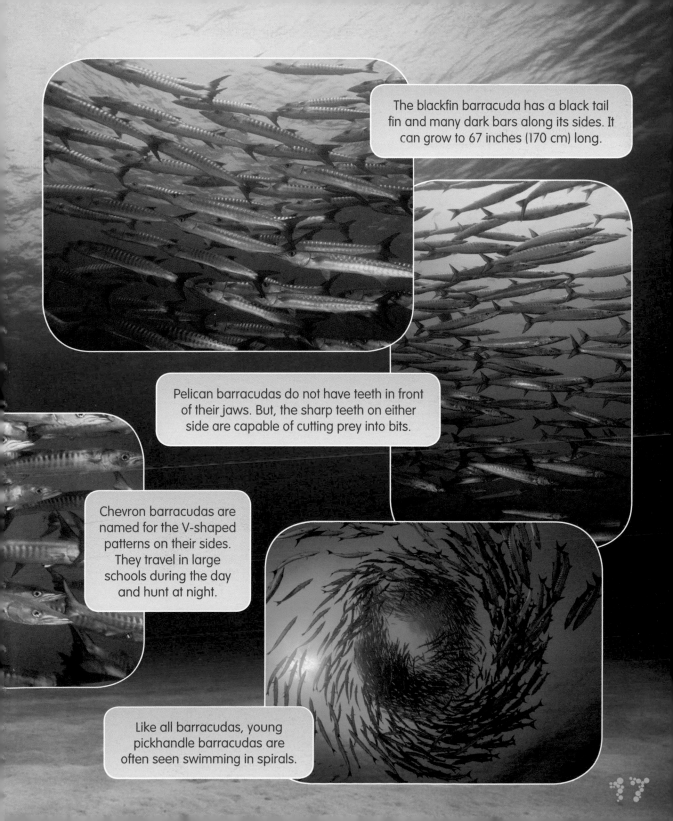

The blackfin barracuda has a black tail fin and many dark bars along its sides. It can grow to 67 inches (170 cm) long.

Pelican barracudas do not have teeth in front of their jaws. But, the sharp teeth on either side are capable of cutting prey into bits.

Chevron barracudas are named for the V-shaped patterns on their sides. They travel in large schools during the day and hunt at night.

Like all barracudas, young pickhandle barracudas are often seen swimming in spirals.

Dinnertime

Barracudas eat many different kinds of fish. Their diet includes anchovies, grunts, groupers, herring, and jacks. Snappers, mullet, and small tuna also make good meals.

Anchovies

Grunts

Herring

Grouper

Barracudas are excellent hunters. They wait for fish to swim by. Then, they use short, speedy movements to surprise and catch their prey.

Sometimes, barracudas swim through schools of fish and slash with their teeth. Then, they quickly turn and feed on hurt fish.

Man-eaters?

Barracudas have been known to bite people. But, most scientists believe that barracudas attack humans by mistake. For example, barracudas may think shiny objects, such as watches, are small fish.

FAST FACTS

Barracudas often follow divers. Some scientists believe the barracudas are hoping the diver is a large predator. A real predator may leave behind food from its own hunt. This makes an easy meal for the barracudas.

Barracudas usually leave divers alone. Still, most divers are careful never to bother barracudas in the wild.

Still, barracudas do have very large teeth. So most divers are very careful when swimming near them. Even one bite from a great barracuda can cause serious harm!

A World Of Danger

Adult barracudas do not have many natural enemies. Goliath groupers, sharks, and tuna sometimes eat small adult barracudas. A variety of fish prey on very young barracudas.

Goliath groupers are one of the largest members of the sea bass family. They can grow to more than eight feet (2 m) long. Some weigh more than 600 pounds (270 kg)!

Humans are a danger to barracudas. Many sport fishermen catch these **aggressive** creatures. Some **commercial** fishing is also aimed at barracudas. But, barracudas are not **endangered**.

Sometimes a fisherman's line breaks during a struggle. When this happens, the hook and line may remain in the barracuda's mouth.

Fascinating Facts

Many people call barracudas "pike of the sea." This is because barracudas resemble freshwater fish called pike. But, pike are not related to barracudas.

Northern pike

Great barracudas are nicknamed "tigers of the sea." Both animals are fast and can be harmful!

The barracuda's fierce nature has inspired many people. In 1964, Plymouth car company presented a car called the Barracuda.

In 1977, the rock group Heart wrote a hit song called "Barracuda." It was in the top 20 on music charts that year.

The Barracuda was a muscle car known for its speed and power.

Learn And Explore

In some areas of the world, people eat barracudas. But most people avoid this meal.

Eating barracudas can lead to ciguatera (see-gwuh-TEHR-uh) poisoning. This illness causes tingling limbs and vomiting. It can also cause headaches, muscle aches, and confusion.

Some fish feed on plants that contain the poison that causes ciguatera. Barracudas become poisonous when they eat these fish.

IMPORTANT WORDS

aggressive displaying hostility.

commercial related to business.

endangered in danger of no longer existing.

fertilize to make fertile. Something that is fertile is capable of growing or developing.

spawn to produce eggs.

species living things that are very much alike.

temperate having neither very hot nor very cold weather.

tropical having warm temperatures.

WEB SITES

To learn more about barracudas, visit ABDO Publishing Company on the World Wide Web. Web sites about barracudas are featured on our Book Links page. These links are routinely monitored and updated to provide the most current information available.

www.abdopublishing.com

INDEX